JOHANN SEBAS[TIAN BACH]

CANTATA

Jesu, der du meine Seele
Jesus, by Thy Cross and Passion
(Dominica 14 post Trinitatis)
for 4 Solo Voices, Chorus and Chamber Orchestra
für 4 Solostimmen, Chor und Kammerorchester
BWV 78

Edited by/Herausgegeben von
Arnold Schering

Ernst Eulenburg Ltd

London · Mainz · Madrid · New York · Paris · Prague · Tokyo · Toronto · Zürich

BACH, CANTATA № 78:
JESU, MY BELOVED SAVIOUR

In the gospel for the 14th Sunday after Trinitatis (Luke, 17, 11—19) the story is told of the healing of the ten lepers. From this Bach's Cantata No. 78 starts out. If only extrinsically. More important than the miracle of that healing, which is only just touched in Nos. 2 and 3, was to Bach's period the reference to the helper- and saviour-province of Christ and, in this connection, to the craving for deliverance of the sinful Christian in general. Thus it does not surprise to find a large number of contrasting affections expressed in the cantata.

The text originates from Johann Rist's church song with the same beginning. Verse 1 and 12 are employed literally Bach's Nos. 1 and 7; a part of the 10th verse in the recitative No. 5) whilst the other original verses have been recomposed into arias and recitatives by an unknown poet (Picander?). The origin of the music falls in the years around 1740.

The opening choral chorus in g minor unfolds an image of seriousness and depression. Bach has given it chaconne form, i. e. he made an incessantly recurring bass theme of four bars the foundation of the development. It appears alternately in the bass (bar 1 seq.), the soprano (9 seq.) or in a middle voice, exceptionally (p. e. bar 25 seq.) even in the reversion. As a musical structure at least 100 years old at that time Bach employs this theme, chromatically descending by a fourth and then cadenced, as a symbol of the sufferings of Christ or, more generally speaking, of mental agony. It is coupled in the beginning (1 seq.) with a chanting countertheme, later (17 seq.) with one stamping upwards in lively rhythms corresponding to the gesture of the „tearing out" of the soul. When the chromatic theme appears in ascending direction (9 seq.) it receives a quaver counterpoint which, however, has instrumental significance only.

The grandeur of the movement is established by two things. Once through the impression caused by the incessantly recurring ostinato theme resembling a mighty mene tekel, and then through the eminent art with which, in spite of this formal compulsion, the choral lines of the soprano are embodied in the entity. It goes without saying that also the three lower voices participate step by step in the interpretation of the text. By this means every single line receives its own expression and its own figurativeness. With an unerring, firm hand the parts are joined, and balanced with respect to their thematic content. No four bars in which there were not something special to admire.

The soprano-alto duet counts to the world-famous solo pieces of the master. Spitta pointed out that the idyllic-delicate character of the music was probably evoked by the second original verse of Rist's song; it speaks of the lambs faithfully in search of Jesus. Everything in this inspired music is set on sheer harmony: the admirable imitation in the solo voices, their pleasant rivalry in the exclamations, their sisterly pairing in chains of thirds and sixths at the end of the sections. Inexpressible, also, the flow of rhythm with most natural declamation. The violoncello indulges in cosy rocking movements and most beautifully supports with the manly quality of its sound the duet of the two lighter human voices.

When this duet — a musical symbol of chastity and purity — has been sung one at first hardly believes the tenor now commencing when he declares the Christians in the bulk as "children of sin". But the orthodox group of the old theology never became tired of emphasizing this again and again. Bach's recitative is full of immense declamatory accents, and with almost alarming impressiveness he hammers word by word into the soul of the hearer. The last bars show the servant of sin in deepest penitence. Actually this is only a psychological device to enable the more effective accentuation of Christ's work of redemption in the following. For already in the next aria (g minor) the soul feels itself disburdened: mild flute tone resounds, and the movement flows easily and without encumbrance. Bach interprets the text line by line. He is especially attracted by the second half of the verse whose strong figurativeness is underlined with tone symbols as subtle as impressive. How inimitably, for instance, the little word "beherzt" (valiant) is embedded in the tonal flow. So great is the delight in the interpretation of militancy and victory that the second part of the aria exceeds the first in length by one half. Hence a da capo is lacking, only the instrumental introduction is repeated.

The tenor aria was probably followed by the sermon. This may have closed with a reference to the passion. Since the bass recitative "The wounds, the nails, the crown and grave" starts out directly from this thought. Again words and conceptions are modeled with flaming passion. It is wonderful how amidst the resting string chords the singing voice loaded with affections jumps about in rugged, jagged lines and how the expression is always reduced to the shortest conceivable formula. No bar in which an inner agitation were not pronounced, no line which were not burdened with a multitude of inner contrasts! In the Andante ("This my heart") really a part of the Matthaeus Passion becomes enlivened: here the ripest Bach pours out the soul of his entire age. Beside the original words of the church-song poem in this place the choral melody is also adopted, if in an expressive, paraphrastic form.

The text of the following aria does not do the poet credit. After this fervently closing recitative one would have wished a different one. "These Now", "So", "Yes", "Since", "When" (Diese Nun, So, Ja, Weil, Wenn) are unmusical words especially when, as here, they march behind oneanother at the beginning of the lines. Beyond this the conceptive substance of the verses is too thin. Even Bach could not make much of them. Since they could not be imbued with real expressiveness he restricted himself to the development of a certain virtuosity. One can hardly term the singing voice more than "adequate". Nevertheless the piece is peculiar for its form. If one notices that the oboe is employed in a strikingly soloistic manner and that the accompanying orchestra persistently throws in the same tutti motive one has the model of a solo-concerto movement. It is not improbable that Bach actually made use of such a movement and adapted it for the cantata by working in the singing voice.

The four-part final choral surprises through its simple harmonisation which — very seldom with Bach — neither enters upon the word "despair" (verzagen) nor upon the phrase "Sin and death do threaten me" (Wenn mich Sünd, und Tod anficht).

Arnold Schering

BACH, KANTATE № 78:
JESU, DER DU MEINE SEELE

Im Evangelium zum 14. Sonntage nach Trinitatis (Luc. 17, 11—19) wird die Heilung der zehn aussätzigen Männer erzählt. Hieran knüpft Bachs Kantate No. 78 an. Freilich nur äußerlich. Wichtiger als das Wunder jener Krankenheilung, das in No. 2 und 3 nur flüchtig gestreift wird, war der Zeit Bachs der Hinweis auf das Helfer- und Retteramt Christi und, damit verbunden, auf die Erlösungsbedürftigkeit des sündigen Christen überhaupt. So überrascht es nicht, in der Kantate eine Menge gegensätzlicher Affekte ausgedrückt zu finden.

Der Text stammt aus Johann Rists Kirchenlied gleichen Anfangs. Strophe 1 und 12 daraus sind wörtlich verwendet (No. 1 und 7 bei Bach; ein Teil der 10. Strophe im Rezitativ No. 5), während die übrigen Originalstrophen durch einen unbekannten Dichter (Picander?) in Arien und Rezitative umgedichtet worden sind. Die Entstehung der Musik fällt in die Jahre um 1740.

Der eröffnende Choralchor in g moll entrollt ein Bild des Ernstes und der Gedrücktheit. Bach hat ihm die Form der Chaconne gegeben, d. h. ein unablässig wiederkehrendes Baßthema von vier Takten zur Grundlage der Entwicklung gemacht. Es erscheint abwechselnd im Baß (Takt 1 ff.), im Diskant (9 ff.) oder in einer Mittelstimme, ausnahmsweise (z. B. 25 ff.) sogar in Umkehrung. Als musikalisches Gebilde damals schon mindestens 100 Jahre alt, benutzt Bach dieses chromatisch um eine Quart abwärtsschreitende und dann kadenzierende Thema als Symbol des Leidens Christi oder, allgemeiner, der Seelennot. Ihm gesellt sich anfangs (1 ff.) ein gesangreiches, später (17 ff.) ein in bewegten Rhythmen aufwärts stampfendes Gegenthema zu, das der Geste des „Herausreißens" der Seele entspricht. Tritt das chromatische Thema in aufsteigender Richtung hervor (9 ff.), so erhält es einen Achtelkontrapunkt, der indessen rein instrumentale Bedeutung behält.

Die Großartigkeit des Satzes wird durch zweierlei bestimmt. Einmal durch den Eindruck, den das immer wiederkehrende, wie ein gewaltiges Menetekel wirkende Ostinatothema macht, und dann durch die hohe Kunst, die trotz dieses formalen Zwangs die Choralzeilen des Soprans in das Ganze hineingebaut sind. Daß darüber hinaus auch die drei unteren Singstimmen schrittweise an der Ausdeutung des Textes teilnehmen, ist selbstverständlich. Auf diese Weise erhält jede einzelne Zeile ihren eigenen Ausdruck und ihre eigene Bildlichkeit. Mit unbeirrbar sicherer Hand sind die Teile aneinandergefügt und auf ihr thematisches Innenleben hin gegeneinander abgewogen. Nicht vier Takte, in denen es nicht etwas Besonderes zu bewundern gäbe!

Das Sopran-Alt-Duett zählt zu den weltberühmten Solostücken des

Meisters. Spitta- hat darauf hingewiesen, daß der idyllisch-zarte Charakter der Musik wahrscheinlich durch die zweite Originalstrophe des Ristschen Liedes hervorgerufen worden ist; dort ist von den Schäflein die Rede, die Jesus treulich suchen geht. Alles an dieser inspirierten Musik ist auf lauteren Wohlklang eingestellt: das entzückende Imitieren der Solostimmen, ihr liebenswürdiger Wetteifer bei den Ausrufen, ihre schwesterliche Paarung in Terzen- oder Sextenketten am Ende der Abschnitte. Unbeschreiblich auch der Fluß im Rhythmischen bei natürlichster Deklamation. In behaglichen Schaukelfiguren ergeht sich das Violoncell und stützt mit der männlichen Färbung seines Klanges aufs schönste den Zwiegesang der beiden helleren Menschenstimmen.

Ist dieses Duett — ein musikalisches Sinnbild der Unschuld und Reinheit — ausgesungen, so glaubt man dem jetzt einsetzenden Tenor zunächst nicht recht, wenn er den Christenmenschen in Bausch und Bogen als „Kind der Sünden" erklärt. Aber die orthodoxe Richtung der alten Theologie wurde nicht müde, dies immer wieder zu betonen. Bachs Rezitativ starrt von gewaltigen deklamatorischen Akzenten, und mit geradezu erschreckender Eindringlichkeit hämmert es Wort um Wort in die Seele des Hörers. Die letzten Takte zeigen die Knechtsgestalt des Sünders in tiefster Zerknirschung. Im Grunde ist dies nur ein psychologischer Kunstgriff, um die Möglichkeit zu haben, die Erlösungstat Christi im folgenden um so wirksamer hervorzuheben. Denn schon in der nächsten A r i e (g moll) fühlt sich die Seele

entlastet: milder Flötenton erklingt, und die Bewegung fließt leicht und ohne Hemmung dahin. Bach legt Zeile für Zeile des Textes aus. Ihn fesselt besonders die zweite Strophenhälfte, deren kräftige Bildlichkeit mit ebenso feinen wie eindrucksvollen Tonsymbolen unterstrichen wird. Wie unnachahmlich ist z. B. das kleine Wort „beherzt" in den Tonfluß eingestellt! Die Freude an der Auslegung des Streitens und Siegens ist so groß, daß der zweite Teil der Arie an Länge den ersten um die Hälfte übertrifft. Infolgedessen fehlt ein Dacapo, nur das instrumentale Vorspiel wird wiederholt.

Wahrscheinlich stand nach der Tenorarie die Predigt. Sie mag mit einem Hinweis auf die Passion geschlossen haben. Denn das B a ß r e z i t a t i v „Die Wunden, Nägel, Kron' und Grab" knüpft unmittelbar an diese Gedanken an. Wiederum sind Worte und Begriffe mit flammender Leidenschaft hingesetzt. Es ist etwas Wunderbares, wie inmitten der ruhenden Streicherakkorde die affektgeladene Singstimme in schroffen, zackigen Linien daherspringt und wie der Ausdruck jedesmal auf die denkbar kürzeste Formel gebracht ist. Kein Takt, in dem sich nicht eine innere Erschütterung ausprägte, keine Zeile, die nicht mit einer Fülle innerer Gegensätze belastet wäre! Beim Andante („Dies, mein Herz") wird geradezu ein Stück Matthäuspassion lebendig: hier spricht reifster Bach die Seele seines ganzen Zeitalters aus. Außer den Originalworten der Kirchenlieddichtung ist an dieser Stelle auch die Choralmelodie mit herübergenommen, freilich in ausdrucksvoll paraphrasierter Gestalt.

Der Text der folgenden Arie spricht nicht zum Lobe des Dichters. Man hätte hinter dem innig schließenden Rezitativ einen anderen gewünscht. Diese Nun, So, Ja, Weil, Wenn sind unmusikalische Worte, zumal wenn sie, wie hier, nacheinander am Anfang der Zeilen aufmarschieren. Auch sonst ist die gedankliche Substanz der Verse nur dünn. Viel konnte selbst Bach mit ihnen nicht anfangen. Da eigentlich Ausdruckshaftes nicht hineinzulegen war, beschränkte er sich auf das Ausspielen einer gewissen Virtuosität. Mehr als „angemessen" wird man die Singstimme kaum nennen können. Dennoch ist das Stück seiner Form wegen eigenartig. Bemerkt man näm-

lich, daß die Oboe in hervorragender Weise solistisch beschäftigt ist, und das begleitende Streichorchester hartnäckig immer das gleiche Tuttimotiv dazwischenwirft, so hat man das Modell eines Solokonzertsatzes vor sich. Es wäre nicht unwahrscheinlich, daß Bach sich tatsächlich eines solchen bedient und unter Einarbeitung der Singstimme ihn für die Kantate nutzbar gemacht hat.

Der vierstimmige S c h l u ß c h o r a l überrascht durch seine schlichte Harmonisation, die — bei Bach sehr selten — weder auf das Wort „verzagen", noch auf die Wendung „Wenn mich Sünd' und Tod anficht" eingeht.

Arnold Schering

BACH, CANTATA No. 78
JESU, DER DU MEINE SEELE
(1740)

Remodelled from libretto of Johann Rist
For the fourteenth Sunday after Trinity

Epistle, Galatians V, 16–24. Walk in the spirit and shun the lusts of the flesh
Gospel, St. Luke XVII, 11–19. Christ heals ten lepers

(Flauto traverso, Corno, 2 Oboes, Organ, 2 Violins, Viola, Cello, Bass and Continuo)

The following English translation of the Cantata has been made by Henry S. Drinker
to be substituted, word for word as indicated, for the original German text throughout
the Cantata. Words and phrases enclosed in parentheses are repeated in the music, for
which use words on the second line. The English text is not copyrighted and may be
used by anyone.

1. Chorus 3/4 (g)

*(Cor. with Soprano; Fl. tr., Ob. I/II,
Strings)*

Je - su, der du mei - ne See - le
Je - sus, by Thy Cross and Pas - sion,

hast durch dei - nen bit - tern Tod,
by the bit - ter pain Thou bore,

aus des Teu - fels finst - rer
when the Ev - il one would

Höh - le und der schwe - ren
hold me deep in Hell to

See - len - not kräf - tig - lich
suf - fer sore, might - i - ly

(her - aus -) ge - ris - sen und
a - way Thou bore me with

(mich sol - ches las - sen wis - sen)
a ha - ven safe be - fore me;

durch dein an - ge - neh - mes
thru Thy Word, con - tent - ment

Wort sei doch jetzt, [O (Gott),
sweet, Thou art still my sure

mein Hort)].
re - treat.

2. Duet Soprano - Alto 4/4 (B)

(Organ and Violoncello; Violone)

Wir ei - len mit schwa - chen, doch
We has - ten with ea - ger yet

em - si - gen Schrit - ten, O Je - su,
fal - ter - ing foot - steps, O Je - sus,

O Mei - ster, zu hel - fen zu dir!
O Mas - ter, for help un - to Thee;

[Du su - chest (die Kran - ken)
Thou faith - ful - ly seek - est
Thou

und Ir - ren - den treu - lich.]
the ill and the err - ing.

Ach hö - re, ach hö - re, ach hö - re,
Ah, hear us, ah, hear us, ah, hear us,

wie wir die Stim - men er - he - ben,
we pray. Our voic - es ex - alt Thee,

(um Hil - fe zu bit - ten!)
for suc - cor we pray Thee,

Es sei uns dein gnä - di - ges
now grant us Thy grac - ious and

Ant - litz (er - freu - lich!)
mer - ci - ful fa - vor!
Thy fa - vor!

(Numbers VI, 25)

3. Recitativo Tenor

Ach! ich bin ein Kind der Sün - den,
Ah! my fail - ings sore - ly grieve me,

ach! ich ir - re weit und breit.
yea, my sins are ve - re great.

Der Sün - den Aus - satz so an mir
The curse of A - dam ne-ver more

zu fin - den, ver - lässt mich nicht
will leave me. so long as I

in die - ser Sterb - lich - keit.
ex - ist in man's es - tate.

Mein Wil - le trach - tet mir nach
My in - cli - na - tions lead to

Bö - sen. Der Geist zwar spricht: ach!
ev - il; tho' oft my soul cries

wer wird mich er - lö - sen?
"Who is there to save me?"

(Romans VII, 24)

A - ber Fleisch und Blut zu zwin-gen
Ah me! to re - sist temp - ta - tion

und das Gu - te zu voll - brin - gen,
and at - tain there-by sal - va - tion

ist ü - ber al - le mei - ne Kraft.
is far be-yond my fee - ble strength.

Will ich den Scha-den nicht ver-heh-len
Tho' I ad - mit my ev' - ry fail-ing,

so kann ich nicht, wie oft ich feh - le,
I find, a - las, the bad in me pre-

zäh - len. Drum nehm' ich nun der
vail - ing. And so I car - ry

Sün - den Schmerz und Pein und mei-ner
to Thy mer - cy -seat my hea-vy

Sor - gen Bür - de, so mir sonst
load of sor - row, with all my

un - er - träg - lich wür - de, und
sions and de - re - lict - ions, and

lief - re sie dir, Je - su, seuf-zend ein,
lay them pen-i - tent-ly at Thy feet.

rech - ne nicht die Mis - se - tat,
Do Thou, Lord, for - give them me,

die dich, Herr, er - zür - net hat.
nor let them yet an - ger Thee.

4. Aria Tenor 6/8 (g) *(Fl. tr.)*

Das (W.)
Dein Blut, so mei - ne Schuld
Thy sac - ri -fice has cleansed

durch-streicht, macht mir das Her - ze
the stain, mak - ing my heart all

wie - der leicht und spricht mich frei,
pure a - gain, hap - py and free,

und spricht mich frei.
hap - py and free.

Ruft mich der Höl - le Herr
Should now the Fiend of Hell

(zum Strei - te,) so ste - het Je - sus
as - sail me, then Thou my Sa-viour

mir zur Sei - te, daß (ich (be - herzt))
will not fail me, but will sup - port

(und sieg - haft) sei.
and suc - cor me.

5. Recitativo Bass *(Strings)*

Die Wun - den, Nä - gel, Kron'
The tor - ments, nail scars, thorns;

und Grab, die Schlä - ge,
the grave, the scourge-marks

so man dort dem Hei - land gab,
that our Lord and Sa - viour bore,

sind ihm nun - meh - ro Sie - ges -
be - come the to - kens of sal -

zei - chen und kön - nen mir
va - tion, to which the Faith -

er - neu - te Kräf - te rei - chen.
ful look for in - spi - ra - tion.

Wenn ein er - schreck - li - ches
When sounds the dread - ed Judg -

Ge - richt den Fluch für die
ment Knell, the curse that sends

Ver - damm - ten spricht, so kehrst
the damned to Hell, turn Thou

du ihn in Se - gen. Mich kann
it in - to bles - sing. Then nei -

kein Schmerz und kei - ne Pein
ther pain nor tor - ment will

♩

be - we - gen, weil sie mein
re - main;   all this my
Hei - land kennt; und da dein Herz
Sa - viour knows, and thus Thy heart
für mich in Lie - be brennt,
with deep af - fect - ion glows;
so le - ge ich hin - wie - der das
so, Mas - ter, I a - dore Thee and
mei - ne vor dich nie - der.
lay my all be - fore Thee.

Dies, mein Herz, mit Leid
This, my heart, with grief
ver - men - get, so dein teu - res Blut
com - min - gled, by Thy prec - ious blood
be - spren - get, so am Kreuz
be sprin - kled on the Cross
ver - gos - sen ist, geb' ich dir,
poured out for me, give I   now,
Herr Je - su Christ.
O Lord, to Thee.

6. Aria Bass 4/4 (c) *(Ob. I, Strings)*

Nun du wirst mein Ge - wis - sen
Do Thou, O Lord, ap - pease my
stil - len,   so wi - der mich
con - science, which grie - vous - ly
(um Ra - che) schreit, da, dei - ne
has trou - bled me; by Thy fi -
Treu - e wird's er - fül - len, weil
de - li - ty up - hold me, and
mir dein Wort (die Hoff - nung) beut.
let Thy Word my com - fort be,

Wenn Chri - sten an dich glau - ben,
by Thy   di - vine di - rect - ion
wird sie (kein Feind in E - wig - keit)
from e - ne - mies for - ev - er   free,
for - ev - er, ev - er   free,
aus dei - nen Hän - den rau - ben.
se - cure in Thy pro - tect - ion.

(St. John X, 28)

7. Chorale 4/4 (g)

(Fl, tr. in 8va, Ob. I, Cor., Vl I with Sop.,
Ob. II, Vl. II with Alto, Vla with Tenor)

Herr, ich glau - be, hilf mir
Lord, I trust Thee, I a -
Schwa - chen, lass mich ja ver - za -
dore Thee, help my weak - ness, my
gen nicht; du,   du kannst mich
de - spair; Thou canst streng - then
stär - ker ma - chen, wenn mich
and re - store me,   when mis -
Sünd' und Tod an - ficht.
deeds my faith in - pair.

Dei - ner Gü - te will ich trau - en,
On Thy lo - ving Grace re - ly - ing,
bis ich fröh - lich wer - de schau - en
God Al - migh - ty glo - ri - fy - ing;
dich, Herr Je - su, nach dem Streit,
by Thy side I hope to be,
in der süs - sen E - wig - keit.
ev - er thru e - ter - ni - ty.

(St. Mark IX, 23)

Jesu, der du meine Seele

Dominica 14 post Trinitatis

Joh. Seb. Bach
1685-1750

3

E.E. 4831

4

hast durch dei - nen bit-tern Tod

Tod, hast durch dei - nen bit-tern Tod

Tod, hast durch dei - nen bit-tern Tod

Tod, hast durch dei-nen bit-tern Tod

6

E. E. 4831

8

E. E. 4831

10

E. E. 4831

12

E. E. 4831

14

Ob.

Vl

Vla.

A.

neh - mes Wort, durch dein an - ge - neh - mes

T.

an - ge - neh - mes Wort, durch dein an-ge-neh-mes

B.

Wort, durch dein an - ge - neh - mes, dein an-ge-neh-mes

C.

5 6 6 5 6 5 7♭ 4♭ 3 6
4 5 4 3

120

Fl.

(forte)

Ob.

forte

Vl.

forte

forte

Vla.

S.

durch dein an-ge-neh-mes Wort:

A.

Wort,durch dein an-ge neh - mes Wort:

T.

Wort,durch dein an-ge neh - mes Wort:

B.

Wort,durch dein an-ge neh - mes Wort:

C.

forte

5 6 7♭ 6 6 6 8 7 6 6 7 7♮ 7 8 7♮
3 4 5 4 4 ♯ 4 4♯ 5♯ 5 4♯ 4♯
2 2 2 2♮ 4 ♯

E. E. 4831

16

19

E. E. 4831

20

E. E. 4831

21

E.E.4831

24

Bösem. Der Geist zwar spricht: ach! wer wird mich er-lö-sen? Aber Fleisch und Blut zu zwingen, und das Gu-te zu voll-brin-gen, ist ü-ber al-le mei-ne Kraft. Will ich den Scha-den nicht ver-heh-len, so kann ich nicht, wie oft ich feh-le, zäh-len. Drum nehm ich nun der Sünden Schmerz und Pein und meiner Sorgen Bürde, so mir sonst unerträglich wür-de, und lief're sie dir, Je-su, seuf-zend ein. Rechne nicht die Mis-se-tat, die dich, Herr, er-zür - - - - - - - - - net hat!

a tempo

E.E. 4831

27

E. E. 4831

Dal Segno

28

RECITATIVO

Die Wunden, Nä-gel, Kron' und Grab, die Schlä-ge, so man

piano e coll'arco

dort dem Heiland gab, sind ihm nunmehro Siegeszeichen, und können mir er-neu-te Kräf-te

Vivace

reichen. Wenn ein erschreckliches Gericht den Fluch für die Verdammten spricht: so

con ardore

E. E. 4831

29

10 Adagio

Vl.

piano

piano

Vla.

piano

Lento

B.

kehrst du ihn in Segen. Mich kann kein Schmerz und keine Pein be-wegen, weil sie mein Hei-land

C.

piano

6   6   4+   7♭   ♭   7♭
♭   5   2   5

Vl.

Vla.

B.

kennt, und da dein Herz für mich in Lie-be brennt, so le-ge ich hin-wie-der das

C.

6   6   4   6♭
4   2
2

Andante

Vl.

Vla.

a tempo

B.

meine vor dir nie - der. Dies, mein Herz, mit Leid ver-men - get,

C.

5♭ 6♭ 6   5   5 6♭ 6   ♭   7   7♭♭ 7♭—6   6   7   5   6 ♮
3   4♭ 3   3   ♭   4   ♮   ♭
2

30

20

so dein_ teu-res Blut be-spren - get, so am Kreuz ver-gos - sen

ist, geb ich dir, Herr Je - su_ Christ.

ARIA

Oboe I

Violino I

Violino II

Viola

Basso

Continuo

piano

E. E. 4831

E.E.4831

85

E.E. 4831

an dich glau - - ben, wird sie kein Feind in Ewigkeit aus deinen Händen rau - - -

- - - - ben, kein Feind in E - - - - - -

E.E. 4831

38